EGON SCHIELE

LUDWIG SCHMIDT

EGON SCHIELE

Translated by Stephen Gorman

This 1991 Edition published by
Zachary Kwintner Books Ltd.
6/7 Warren Mews, London W1P 5DJ
ISBN 1 872532 41 1
Printed in Germany – Imprimé en Allemagne

CONTENT

Schiele had wandered through the wakeful day as a dreamer and visionary and had carried with him a dream which spreads out infinitely. Life had burdened him with much suffering, letting a man who was incredibly sensitive experience life, and only art gave him delight through the work which it caused. This is the reason why he worked with an insatiable greed, with an almost unprecedented indefatigability.

Arthur Roessler

THE ARTIST IN HIS ERA

A new intellectual climate inspired the young generation of artists after the turn of the century. The call for inner truth and simplicity in art could not be ignored. Popular art had had little to do with reality for a long time, in a world of false decoration the most unusual effects had been produced. The more the omens of the catastrophe of World War I could be anticipated, the more susceptible and fragile became the conventional understanding of art. Especially in Vienna, described by Karl Kraus as the test station for the end of the world, there was a rapid development towards the fall of the Austrian-Hungarian monarchy.

Three artists became central figures of the artistic development in Vienna at the turn of the century. Gustav Klimt was the oldest of the three. Egon Schiele was the second oldest, while Oskar Kokoschka, as the youngest of the three artists, was able to carry Viennese modern art well into the 20th century.

Gustav Klimt had still learned the intellectual basis of the main art style of that era, historical painting, from its most outstanding representative, Hans Makart. Klimt was employed by Makart's studio as a young helper and in the beginning given menial work. As a prospective artist he took on tasks which the old Makart was incapable of and finally the maturing master was given commissions which Makart had been unable to complete due to his death. Klimt detached himself from these beginnings and with his increasing artistry completed the transition to modern art step by step, brought elements of an individual style of Art Nouveau into his art and in his later works even took the decisive step towards expressionism.

When Egon Schiele entered the art scene in Vienna, Klimt was the undisputed central figure. He only just touched the Art Nouveau style, allowed his artistic volition to be influenced by Klimt but went his own individual way to expressionism.

Oskar Kokoschka finally began as an unruly young man with a consistent expressionistic style. He was backed by Klimt although this artist was never quite able to fully understand the acts of the impetuous young man. He eventually left Vienna, hallmarked as the great hope of modern Viennese art and, at the same time, as the enfant terrible of the visual arts.

Vienna was decisively weakened in its artistic potency through Kokoschka's departure and through the deaths of Schiele and Klimt. It sunk into provincialism. This was certainly not just a sign of artistic decline. The breaking apart of the empire as a result of World War I also plunged the city into complete meaninglessness from a political point of view: the decline from being the splendid capital of an empire to becoming an inflated metropole of a small European country was too rapid.

Before this decline, Vienna had been a fertile breeding ground which held all the various sediments necessary for a radical change. Klimt still found an individual way to a pretentious art in an area rich in tension between Art Nouveau with its formal obligations and expressionism which was strongly expressive. It was a very impressive path which was admittedly only open to him as the last of a great era. Klimt died leaving no students, his way had led to an end-point. The young artists who came after him could admire his art, but were unable to follow it. They had to go the far more difficult, modern and strictly radical path towards expressionism, where symptoms of sickness in western cultural existence broke out everywhere and chasms opened up in daily life as well as in the mind. There was a reason why psychoanalysis was developed in Vienna in those years. The darker areas of human inner life which lay on the other side of the threshold of consciousness were discovered and burdened life with the knowledge of the uncontrollable instinctive subconscious.

For the Secession artists the outer cover, an extensive building, in a style which suited the paintings which were to be presented there, was still a main desire. The lifestyle around the turn of the century was characterized by an extravagant ambience. The Vienna of 1870 was the centre of a striving middle-class which was given a lot of free space by a royal family who proceeded cleverly. Historicism, not as an artistic style but as a theoretical model, was simply ubiquitous in this city and had to lead to a great degree of bold conception. For example, in Vienna the Ringstrasse was created with buildings which were copied from all imaginable styles of the past. Style was a vital question. Official buildings were designed one after the other. The Gothic plain city hall as a symbol of clearly organized middle-class desire, the House of Parliament presented itself in a solemn Greek style, the university in the enlightened

spirit of the Renaissance and finally, as an expression of baroque joy of life, the Burgtheater: adaptations of past cultural epochs for the respective areas of use.

The Secession, as a group of artists willing to change, was not long established, when the need was felt for a proper building for the presentation of their art. The building had to be conceived even before a style could be formed. It is no wonder that the spirit of the Secession was at first the common desire to establish new art forms from this era instead of reproduced styles of history. Much has been said about the Secession style, but strictly speaking no such style existed. There were individual attempts at new forms, but almost all of the young artists created their own awakening to a new era. It was significant that artistic programmes were only manifested with vague phrasing, where it was only clear that one wanted something new, while the leading heads immediately went ahead to find adequate exhibition premises for their art. No sooner was the Secession called to life than Gustav Klimt occupied himself intensively with the plan for an exhibition building. The building was designed by Joseph Maria Olbrich in the spirit of a renewed architecture: he formed the outer shell for a movement of artistic awakening which was conscious of the necessity of new directions and new aims, however, a clear »where« was missing. Klimt was an inspired innovator, Schiele an individual driven by basic artistic instincts, Kokoschka was chaotic, he needed the destructive decomposition in order to create something new. All the other artists among the Secessionists were individualists or lacked the final artistic potency. »Their conviction led them away from historicism which they found anachronistic to investigate new ideas in all their European forms of appearance. Jugendstil and Art Nouveau, French impressionism and Belgian naturalism found eager interest among the Secessionists, since it was the young artists who brought the European artistic developments to Vienna.« (E. Mitsch) The young Schiele was able to study the development of modern art in Europe in Vienna. Klimt and his fellow artists had obtained their exhibition by force. Paintings by van Gogh and the impressionists, by Munch and Picasso were accessible to Schiele as solutions for possible artistic problems, and he used them accordingly. Admittedly a sure stylistic support on which he could base his own artistic achievements did not exist. One could not deduce any guidelines from the general awakening to new aims. The young Schiele had to discover completely new ideas for himself. What the others could give him was only the knowledge that the artists of the new age could and must be open and that he was allowed to realize the artistic statements which struggled to get out in any form whatsoever in a painting. This was a fantastic challenge for a truly great and brilliant talent. However, to a sensitive young man, burdened by his origins and characteristics, it also gave the feeling of being thrown into a brutal world.

Edvard Munch, the expressionist who came from the north, created with his representation »The Scream« the key picture of an epoch and the style which was a result of the necessity of this era: the original expressionistic painting. The same existential state of emergency moved the artist Egon Schiele. »The shock to the belief in a godly system of the world had as a result, apart from a deep isolation, that fateful, unrestrained subjectivism which had complete trust in almost nothing but the primary sources of the individual ego. The consciousness of being at someone's mercy and being without a home provokes a situation of anxiety, one of the most important basic experiences of the expressionists' generation. It is very strongly tied to the question of the meaning of life, which is also the central concern of psychoanalysis.« (E. Mitsch)

The young artists after the turn of the century endeavoured to find radical separation from the usual stiff, hollow style of painting. However, they also distanced themselves from the aesthetic play of form of Art Nouveau with its overdone refinement after touching it more or less strongly. Originality and primitiveness, a return to the roots of art took its place. Beside this one finds a definite social commitment. The expressionistic artists partly turned to the world of the working people, where, admittedly, they encountered crass misunderstanding and rejection. The worlds of progressive art and hard factory labour were too far apart. Man is the main focus of the new art, the central point of work is the struggle for one's daily bread.

For the young artists intention was more decisive than external influences. The external nature of objects is raw material, encouragement for the presentation of one's own visions. A new language of form had to be developed from a consciously revolutionary spirit, as the media of presentation up to this time did not suffice for the attainment of the high aims.

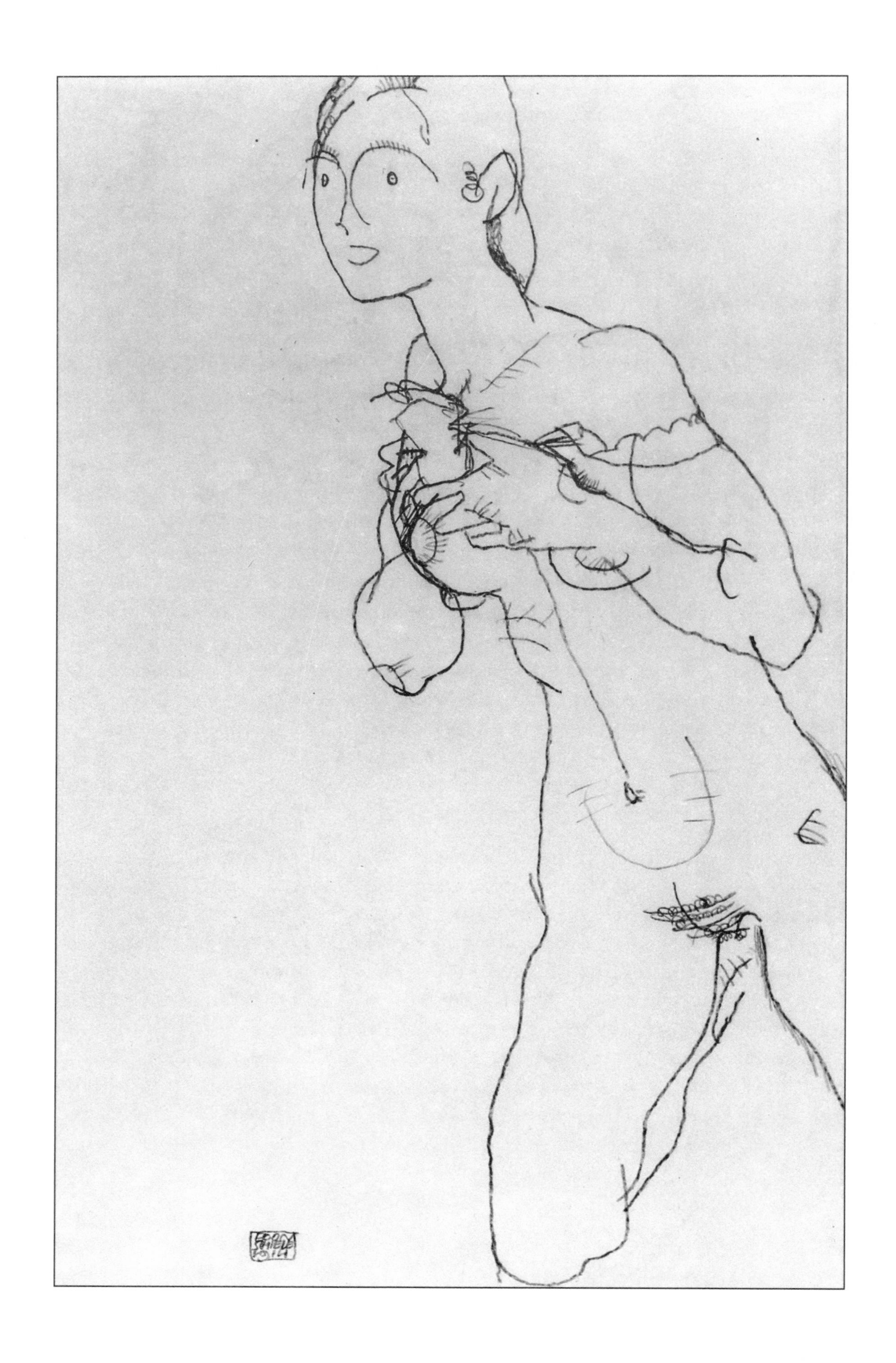

THE ARTIST'S LIFE

Egon Schiele was born on June 12th, 1890, the son of an Austrian railway official, in the lower Austrian small town of Tulln on the Danube. His father was principal of the railway station, the family home was bourgeois and restricting. His father died under quite oppressive circumstances, when the boy Egon was fourteen years old. It is thought today that he suffered from progressive paralysis. His sister Gertrude who was six years younger meant more than anyone else to the young boy. She was the confidante of his younger years and later appeared quite often as one of his first models.

Egon Schiele qualified from primary school and then transferred to the secondary school in Krems. However, he left there soon afterwards and attended the school in Klosterneuburg where his scholastic abilities were certainly not outstanding. After his father's death his uncle and godfather Leopold Czihaczek was appointed as guardian. Being a technician himself, he imagined his ward studying at the technical college, but the bad notes in school proved to be a hindrance. However, two art teachers in Klosterneuburg as well as an artist who lived there had recognized the unusual artistic talent of the young pupil and smoothed the way for the entrance examination to the art academy in Vienna. What the young man was able to present there impressed the examining committee so much that his acceptance to the academy was recommended and Schiele was in fact admitted.

He attended the painting class of Professor Griepenkerl. Almost all the Viennese artists of that time who had academy training had been taught by this rather inflexible man. Egon Schiele could not harmonize with his professor in spite of the enthusiasm with which he had begun his new career. After two years he accepted the consequences and left the academy together with several fellow students whose early »break for freedom« did not suit them quite as well from an artistic point of view as it did Schiele. They all joined together in a group of young artists, called themselves »Neukunstgruppe« and were soon given the opportunity of exhibiting their work, but Schiele was the only one who stood out in the group. Gustav Klimt and his friends had left the Secession in 1905 because they no longer agreed with its aims and exhibition methods. One of the results was that the Secession building was no longer available to them for exhibition purposes. The architect Josef Hoffmann improvised on an empty building site — the site where the concert hall stands today — an adequate temporary exhibition area which in 1908 and 1909 was able to present the great »Kunstschau«, organized by the Klimt group.

The show of 1908 was dedicated to Austrian art. For Schiele the encounter with the famous Klimt paintings, which he probably had never seen before, must have been an experience. The show created a certain sensation by showing a cabinet with works by the angry young man Oskar Kokoschka. Klimt had insisted that Kokoschka was given the opportunity of presenting his paintings. When he was attacked because of this decision, he spoke decisively in favour of the young Kokoschka, »We are obliged to give a great talent the possibility of expression. Oskar Kokoschka is the greatest talent of the young generation. And even if we are in danger of having our art exhibition demolished, one can do nothing about it. But we will have done our duty.« Kokoschka's paintings were a sensation. »For three of his wall-sized sketches,« wrote the critic Ludwig Hevesi about Kokoschka's exhibition contribution, »he would be torn apart in the air, but that would do him and the sky some good . . .«

The 1909 exhibition was dedicated to the international connections in modern art. It was a moving experience for Egon Schiele to have his work accepted for this exhibition. Suddenly he saw his work combined with that of the great personalities of the art world in one exhibition. His pictures were shown together with works from Oskar Kokoschka who did not think much of Schiele. Schiele's as well as Kokoschka's contributions were taken very little notice of by the public and the critics. Kokoschka, whose exhibits had been the sensation of the show in the previous year, placed the blame for the disinterest on Schiele. He was in no way favourably disposed towards Schiele and also in later years made various disparaging remarks about him.

It was decisive for Schiele's progress that several collectors had noticed him and that the art critic Arthur Roessler discovered him. In the following years he played a great part in publicizing the young talent. Arthur Roessler was the art critic for the Arbeiter Zeitung. When he had recognized Schiele's talent he dedicated a considerable amount of his publishing space to the young artist. Soon a deep friendship developed between the two, and Schiele took considerable advantage of this relationship by drawing the other in to settle the catastrophies which constantly threatened his life. Whether it was financial help or extensive errands at awkward times, the supervision of his paintings or dealing with over-sensitive collectors: Roessler was asked to help time and time again. It does the journalist honour that even after it came to a quarrel which ended the personal contact, he did not cease expressing the importance of the artist in his publishing work, even after Schiele's death.

The art exhibition of 1909 showed a choice selection of works by great European painters and the knowledge of these paintings was an important experience for all Viennese artists. Pierre Bonnard and Maurice Denard represented the Nabis from Paris, there were paintings from Gauguin and van Gogh beside Henri Matisse and — especially important — Edvard Munch. Jan Toorop was already well-known in Vienna as was Felix Vallotton.

Schiele's paintings were shown beside paintings from this illustrious circle. However, more important for his fame was an exhibition which took place in the Gallery Pisko through Arthur Roessler's mediation. Here, the young people from the Neukunstgruppe could present their paintings. In the Viennese art scene at that time it was an unusual event. Normally it was almost impossible in Vienna for young and unknown artists to obtain possibilities for exhibiting. The few private galleries were concerned with presenting successful, i.e. saleable artists, all the other associations were only open to members. And one could only become a member when one could show that one was successful.

Through the exhibition and Arthur Roessler's mediation Schiele got to know two of the most important collectors of art in Vienna: Carl Reininghaus and Dr. Oskar Reichel. Schiele's entry to the Viennese art scene was unusually successful and by comparison financially secure, something which very few young artists could claim in Vienna. However, the young man's personality was not equal to his external success. In the following years Schiele got entangled in an unending chain of problems and difficulties which brought him physical and psychical problems. Vienna, where he had just started to achieve success, became from one day to the next unbearable for him. In 1910, he wrote to his friend Anton Peschka, »I want to leave Vienna very soon. How awful it is here. Everyone is treacherous and jealous of me: former colleagues smile falsely at me. In Vienna is shadow, the city is black, I need a cure. I want to be alone. I want to go to the Bohemian Forest. May, June, July, August, September, October: I must see something new and investigate it. I wish to taste dark water, cracking trees, to see wild air, to stare at

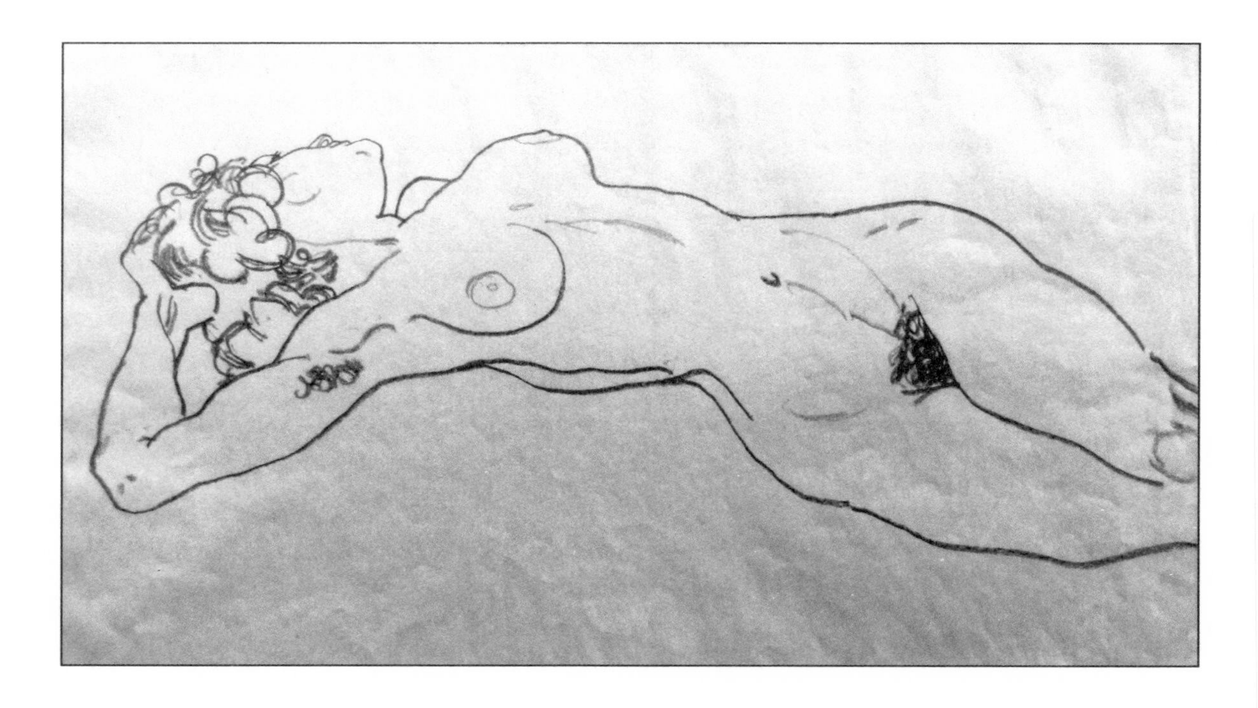

rotting fences, how they all live, to hear young birch groves and quivering leaves, I want to see light and sun, to enjoy wet green evening vales, to sense the goldfish shining, to see white clouds forming. I want to talk to the flowers. To look at grass, rose-coloured people, old dignified churches, to hear small cathedrals speaking. I want to walk on and on without stopping on round mountainous fields, through wide open plains, I want to kiss the earth and smell soft warm moss: then I will form beautiful coloured areas.«

Schiele left Vienna. He went to Krumau in southern Bohemia where his mother had been born. He had no contact with his relatives though. For a time he was completely under the spell of a very dubious character, the painter Erwin Osen who had a bad influence on Schiele. Osen came to Krumau in the company of the dancer Moa, »a very slender dancer... The staring, large, dark, flashing eyes under brown-blue shadowed, long lashes and heavy lids, the guttural, cooing voice... entranced the artist in Schiele completely...« reported Arthur Roessler on the encounter.

In Krumau, Schiele also lived together with Wally Neuzil who he had become acquainted with as a model and who became a close friend for a long time. It soon became obvious that he could not carry on his city way of life without problems: He was accused of being too friendly with the village children who he used as models and he was criticized for living together with Wally without being married. All this eventually forced him to move away. After a short interlude in Vienna he moved to Neulengbach where he felt content and carried on living as in Krumgau, but his tendency to use little girls from the area as models almost cost him his freedom. It was never proved whether Schiele actually did commit indecent assault on the children or whether their immature bodies were necessary for the presentation of his artistic expression. However, Schiele was charged, imprisoned and convicted. It was said that one of his sketches was burned in the trial, but one cannot be sure of this. The proceedings and the whole degrading situation deeply affected the artist who was already shaken by crisis.

Soon after this low in his life Schiele had a recovery. He gained new customers and his financial situation improved. Gustav Klimt wanted to cheer him up and help him after his shattering spell in prison. He recommended him to the Lederer family who already possessed a considerable part of Klimt's works and who had the means which enabled them to be kindly disposed to yet another artist. He was invited to the family seat in Györ to carry out a portrait commission. It was a stay rich in atmosphere which heartened him more than one can imagine.

The foreboding political clouds over Europe and especially over Vienna were obvious to the sensible, sensitive Egon Schiele long before the outbreak of World War I and the tense atmosphere caused him great difficulties, something which is obvious in his work.

The outbreak of war in 1914 did not come as a surprise to him, the war first interfered with his life one year later. Because of his weak constitution he was freed from active military service and was only called up for service in the military administration in 1915. A few days before he began, he married Edith Harms, with whom he had been friends for quite a while before. When Schiele was drafted to Prague, his wife followed him there, in fact she was close to him for the whole duration of the war. The first military training was one of the most difficult times in his life. After his basic training he was employed in different places in the vicinity of Vienna with various administrative tasks. Before the war Schiele had been drawn to the countryside, now he did everything possible in order that he could be drafted to Vienna so that he would be close to the general art scene. In 1917 he was eventually successful. Friends had managed to have him posted to the Imperial-Royal Consumer Establishment for the Salaried in the Army in the Field, an official name which only a group of veteran civil servants could have invented. The office was equally antiquated, however, among the higher officials were a number of art admirers and Schiele was able to continue painting in the shadow of this war office.

At the beginning of 1918, Gustav Klimt died, the great master of the Viennese art scene. With his death Schiele became number one among the Viennese artists since Oskar Kokoschka sulkingly stayed away from his hometown. Interesting commissions, considerable offers of exhibitions and the task which he had suddenly been given, of being at the head of the artists on many occasions, helped him to work a lot. Again Schiele received a military transfer, he was drafted to the army museum. With this he seemed to have received a post which was most removed from the war. However, for the last months he had a secret fear that he would suddenly be removed from Vienna by the military administrative machinery.

The last months of the war became more difficult for the population. Food provisions became worse and worse, the daily struggle for survival more and more difficult. In autumn 1918 there was a severe influenza epidemic in Vienna and many people were affected. In October Edith Schiele became ill and died on October 28th of Spanish Influenza. Schiele also became ill and died a few days after his wife on October 31st at an age when an artist is normally said to be at the start of his career. Schiele was undoubtedly an early completer. However, it is sad that his life was ended at a time when he would have had the peace ahead of him for creating great works of art.

THE ARTIST'S WORK

When Egon Schiele successfully completed the entrance examination for the academy of graphic art as a sixteen year old, he proved his great artistic talent while during his school years he had been a very bad pupil. His achievements at the academy also left a lot to be desired. In fact the decision to attend the academy was a mistake. Schiele's original wish and the recommendation of his patron from Klosterneuburg had been acceptance in the school for arts and crafts. However, the professors in this institute which was considerably below the status of the academy felt that the disposition of the young Schiele was sufficient for the higher orders of the academy, and so they passed the applicant on with a recommendation. The fact was, however, that the training at the academy was sterile and everything else but beneficial for a talent like Schiele's. While Professor Griepenkerl had his pupils work completely in a conservative, traditional style, a group of young people formed in the arts and crafts school who could go their own way relatively freely. This led them directly to the circle of artists around Klimt and offered them several chances of employment within the framework of the »Wiener Werkstätte«.

Soon after his admission to the academy in Vienna, Schiele sought contact to Gustav Klimt, the outstanding artistic personality in the Viennese scene. Getting to know the person as well as his work was certainly not easy. Klimt lived a secluded life, was concerned only with his work and was very taciturn regarding his art; there are very few statements passed down from him concerning his work. Klimt was an exceptionally slow, thoughtful painter, his works are relatively few and even during his lifetime collector friends eagerly awaited the completion of work, which was already bought, to add to their collections immediately after delivery. One could hardly see work from Klimt apart from in the exhibitions which were few and far between. The artist regularly had to borrow paintings from his collectors for these shows. These exhibitions were therefore the only opportunity for the young Schiele to see works from Klimt. It was different with Klimt's sketches. The artist painted slowly but sketched quickly. One can see this from the innumerable hand drawings which he left. Admittedly Klimt retained most of his sketches, declared only a few valid and let them go as signed works. Schiele must have therefore been highly delighted at the interest shown by the great master when, after only a short friendship, he was offered the opportunity of exchanging sketches, a show of trust which Klimt did not extend to many people.

Schiele's first Viennese years were a time under Klimt's spell. What the academy had to offer had almost no effect on the artistic personality which was forming. His apathetic academy tasks were at the most average, he painted the compulsory exercises so insignificantly as if he was an untalented artisan like so many others. At the same time the expressionist in him who was already struggling for an inner truth developed, although he still formally obtained his qualifications in Klimt's wake. Internally he was already fighting deep-seated problems which forced an expressionism with a completely individual character, away from the art of the Secession.

He was given his first liberation to an individual style by impressions from a foreign world, as he travelled to Trieste with his sister. In the ship paintings from the Mediterranean the typical Schiele colours are mixed with obvious Art Nouveau elements.

Thematically completely in connection with Klimt, the first version of the painting »Water Spirits« was created in 1907, which admittedly is of a severe geometric formation instead of the supple, cat-like, elegant, female figures which enliven Klimt's picture »Watersnakes«. Where Klimt shows bewitching sensuality in rich colour, the same theme is shown by Schiele in a graphically unheard of exciting, but also stern, almost demure way. Schiele began to go his own way: a second version of the painting from 1908 shows clearly the swift development of the artistic hand. From a colour point of view Schiele was to use large areas for a long time, reduced to almost monochrome coloured details similar to coloured building bricks. He achieved the greatest effects with the most economical use of media.

The year 1910 brought a decisive breakthrough in Egon Schiele's work. What the artist had done up until then had been tentative searching, experiments in finding his own path, suggestions from the respected master Klimt. Now Schiele had taken in the art of the Secession and altered it to expressionism. From then on his work was a beacon, an eruptive outbreak of spontaneous and elementary creative power. The twenty year old went his own way uncompromisingly towards a new expressive art, where none of his colleagues from the academy could follow. Schiele began to deform the bodily features of his models in order to make inner conditions of the soul externally visible.

Inner struggles were made apparent through this, »mimic games and theatrical gestures were exaggerated to morbid tensions, which were no more subject to will and could no longer be controlled by it. Ferdinand Hodler understood how to flood his figures with elemental power streams as very few artists at the start of the century did. With Schiele this movement freezes and coagulates as in a cramp.« (Erwin Mitsch)

One has to realize that the young Schiele, because of his background, previous blows of fate and his individual personality, appeared in no way to have the prerequisites for a strong solo attempt in the history of western art. Physically and psychically he had been tossed around and was rather incapable of wresting the necessary creative peace for artistic greatness from his outer way of life. He was prepared to develop a completely new art in a time of complete artistic change, in a quality which almost no one believed the still very immature Schiele capable of. At the same time this art in its individual stages is for an unprepared contemporary completely incomprehensible. Looking back at the life's work of an artist one has a very different view than when one is confronted with a few works at the time of their creation. Admittedly there were a few people who saw the artist's format or at least suspected it. Schiele was able to come closer to a few of them with portraits since he dedicated himself intensively to portrait painting around 1910. However, the painting of the great inspirer, the architect Otto Wagner, remained unfinished. But others, e.g. the pictures of Arthur Roessler and Eduard Kosmack, clearly show how different and new Egon Schiele's art became. Tenseness in the figures, exciting compositions, hands deliberately placed in seismographical positions make inner conditions externally visible. With their symbolic character gestures, pose and intensive looks resemble ciphers.

The same significant attitude can also be found in paintings which have themes concerned with the spirit of the age. The painting of his dead mother from 1911 is among those, a theme which many artists chose in those years. Hodler and Klimt, Munch and many others created this theme. The contrast between life and death is also the central statement of the picture with Schiele. The comparison between the woebegone dead body and the still partially unformed figure of the child shown in a suprasensuous light. In the painting »Pregnant Woman and Death« the child is also a bright figure in a dark picture with no light coming from the outside. Schiele was quite willing to allow symbols of human existence in landscape and nature paintings to shine through or to include them as documentary evidence of the inner credibility of the

painting. The »Dead City« is one of those paintings full of symbols and even the »Autumn Trees« from 1911 in their triad form can be seen in relation to the events on Golgatha (the Crucifixion).

Until 1913 the tree landscape again took an increasingly important place in Schiele's work, since it offered his tendency to see things in a symbolistic way special room for expression. In this connection the close interrelationship between nature and man must be mentioned. Schiele's nudes and Schiele's trees emanate from a common view of special experiences: he weaves together the visible and invisible things in his paintings and experiences the outer and inner world as a universal cosmos. »Now I mainly observed the bodily movement of mountains, water, trees and flowers. Everywhere one is reminded of similar movements in the human body, of similar motions of joy or suffering in the plants.«

The year 1915 brought for the artist, on the one hand, an end to his overexcited state of mind, on the other hand, a considerable reduction in the amount of free time which he had. His marriage to Edith Harms produced a social binding for his unsteady life and an orientation of his seeking. However, four days after his wedding, Schiele was called up for military service in Prague, later he was posted close to Vienna. His wife followed him to the respective postings, but his artistic work was impeded because of the new situation.

Schiele had kept up an intensive study of the self-portrait throughout his whole lifetime. Phases of severe mental strain can be seen in the tragic conflicts around his physical self. The portraits from 1915 still show the artist as an oversensitive person living under almost unbearable tension. During the year his personality underwent a change: he felt relieved of the inhibitions of his previous existence. The new attitude towards life was clearly shown in the life-size painting of his wife in a coloured dress, which radiates an immense harmony.

Egon Schiele's nude paintings were also closely connected to the self-portraits. In the years of inner struggle when he was full of despair, he painted cramped and tense figures, bony people in inhumanly distorted positions. At other times the nude paintings were struggles with Eros, clear encoded conflicts with sexuality. Later he placed articles of clothing on his nudes, who were all painted from models. They served more as accessories to emphasize the nakedness rather than hide it.

In 1917, he painted loving couples united in love in a relaxed pose, with no inner torture. The peak of his nude paintings was his probably most popular painting the »Family«, completed in 1918, in which he leads the representation of corporeality away from the level of erotic presentation to the blissful togetherness of a group of people united by love. »After the representation of erotic love affairs between the sexes follows the logical extension of the theme to the family, a contemplation of the intrinsic tasks and roles of man and woman.« (E. Mitsch)

Schiele's lifelong publishing companion, his long standing friend Arthur Roessler, never tired of trying to free Schiele's artistic personality from the false reputation of being a manic erotic. Once he wrote, »It certainly should not be denied that his mystic, spiritualized religiousness sometimes drove Schiele spontaneously to eroticism and that he became a horror figure for all the hypocritical, moralizing Philistines; but as he had very swiftly passed the test of absurdity in the spiritual academy of the revolutionary — where he had learned to express the uncorrect correctly — one could eventually take the trouble not to see exclusively the ecstatic paintings of figures created in a certain period of his development, which appear to have been born in angry convulsions from a mixture of prevented or degenerated sexuality and the excruciating tremors of suffering souls, but to turn one's attention to the modest and tender landscapes and figure compositions of his later years.«

The last two years of his life brought recognition of Schiele's work and — because of numerous portrait commissions money for a comfortable life. Apart from the paintings of his wife, the »Portrait of Albert Paris Gütersloh« with its complete perfection is very important. It gives the impression that the artist had found the key to a continuous further life's work of the highest quality with this painting, when his sudden death brought his work to a tragic end while he was still so young.

ILLUSTRATIONS

Sailing Boats in Undulating Water (Trieste). 1907
Oil on pencil drawing on top of cardboard, 25 x 18 cm
Neue Galerie der Stadt Graz

SCHIELE
EGON.
07.

Gerti Schiele. 1909

Oil on canvas, 140.5 x 140 cm

Private collection

Autumn Tree. 1909

Oil on canvas, 89 x 89 cm
Hessisches Landesmuseum, Darmstadt

Self-Portrait with Outspread Fingers. 1909

Oil and golden bronze colours on canvas, 71.5 x 27.5 cm
Private collection

S. 10.

S.10.

S.10.

MOA

MOA

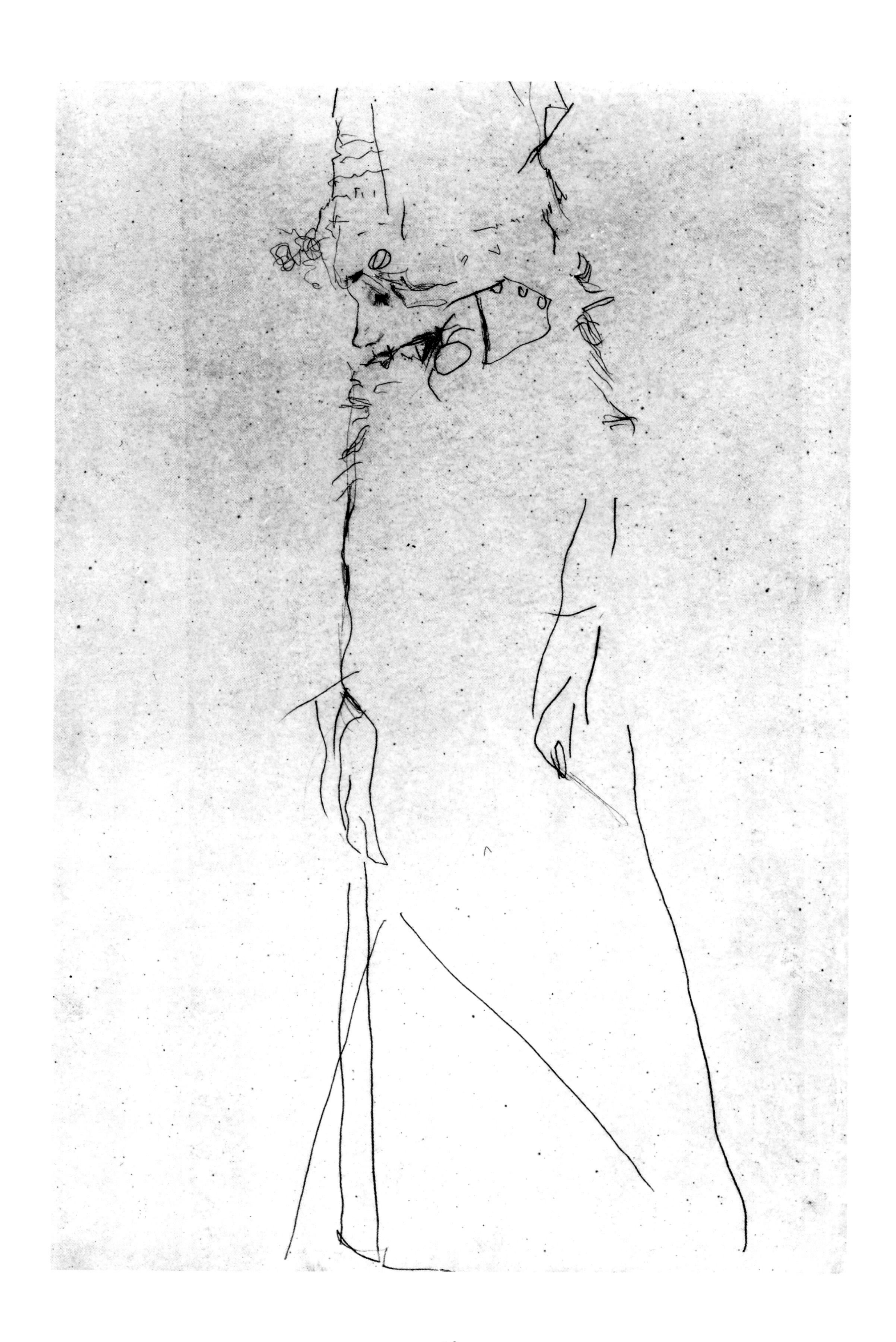

EGON
SCHIELE
1911

Sunflower. 1909/10

Oil on canvas, 150 x 29.8 cm

Historisches Museum der Stadt Wien, Vienna

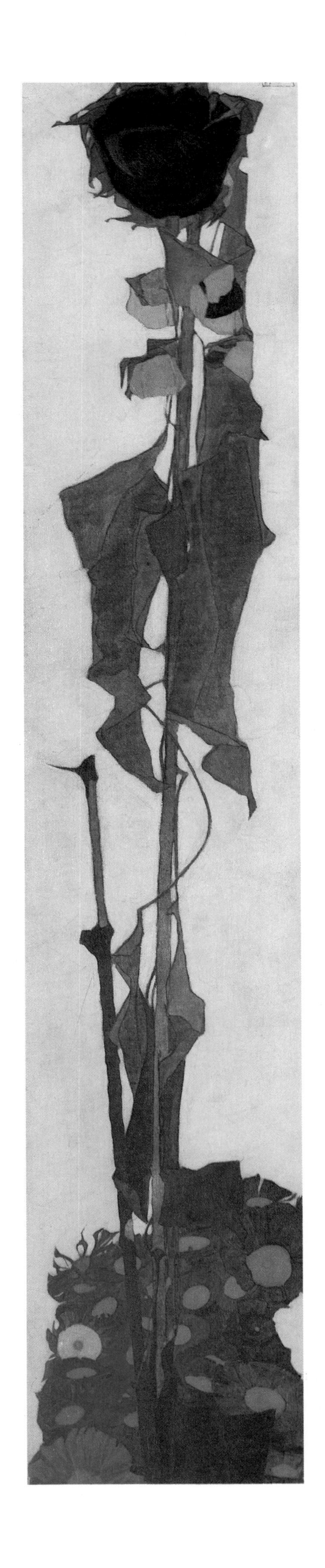

Autumn Trees I. 1911

Oil on canvas,

79.5 x 80 cm Sammlung Hans Dichand, Vienna

Female Nude on Coloured Blanket. 1911
Pencil, aquarelle, 48 x 31 cm
Neue Galerie der Stadt Graz

EGON
SCHIELE
1911

Self-Portrait. 1911

Oil on wood, 27.5 x 34 cm
Historisches Museum der Stadt Wien, Vienna

EGON
SCHIELE
1911.

Sunflowers. 1911

Oil on canvas, 90.4 x 80.5 cm
Österreichische Galerie, Vienna

EGON
SCHIELE
1911

Pregnant Woman and Death. 1911
Oil on canvas, 100.3 x 100.1 cm
Nationalgalerie, Prague

Madonna. 1911

Oil on canvas, 79.5 x 80.3 cm
Sammlung Hans Dichand, Vienna

Dead City. 1912
Oil on canvas, 80 x 80 cm
Kunsthaus, Zurich

EGON
SCHIEL
1912

EGON
SCHIELE
1912.

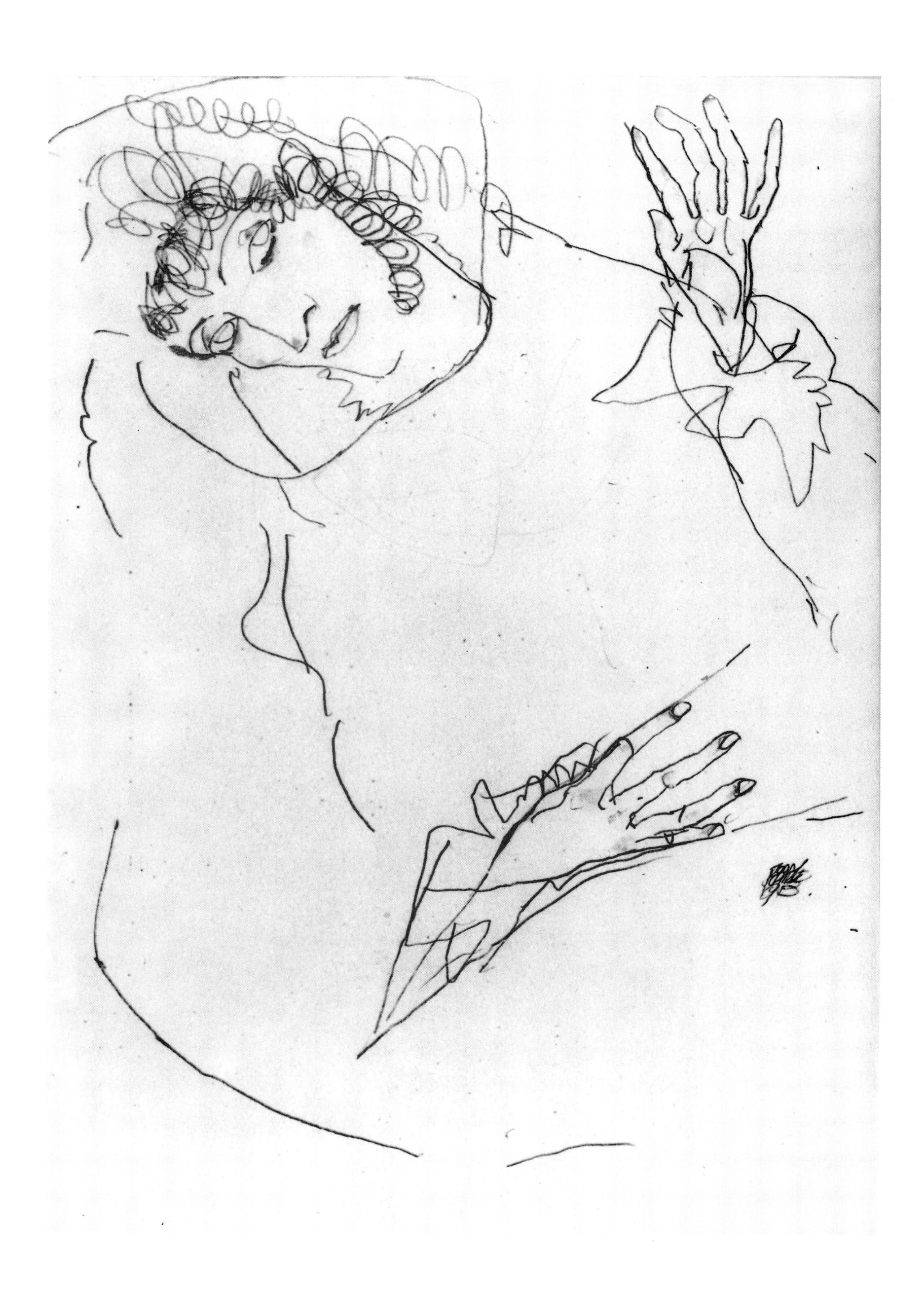

EGON

Agony. 1912
Oil on canvas, 70 x 80 cm
Neue Pinakothek, Munich

EGON
SCHIELE
1912

Self-Portrait with Raised Arms. 1913

Black crayon, aquarelle and opaque colours on paper, 48 x 31.5 cm
Sammlung Hans Dichand, Vienna

Portrait of Trude Engel. 1913

Oil on canvas, 100 x 100 cm

Neue Galerie der Stadt Linz, Wolfgang-Gurlitt-Museum

Double Portrait of Heinrich and Otto Benesch. 1913
Oil on canvas, 121 x 129.9 cm
Neue Galerie der Stadt Linz, Wolfgang-Gurlitt-Museum

Nude Back of Girl with Long Plait

Pencil, aquarelle and opaque colours,
47.7 x 32 cm Sammlung Hans Dichand, Vienna

EGON
SCHIELE
1913

Window Wall. 1914

Oil on canvas, 110 x 140 cm
Österreichische Galerie, Vienna

Suburb. 1914

Canvas on hardboard, 101 x 120.5 cm
Staatsgalerie, Stuttgart

EGON
SCHIELE
1917

Woman with Orange Stockings. 1914

Pencil, aquarelle and opaque colours on paper, 48.1 x 31.9 cm
Sammlung Hans Dichand, Vienna

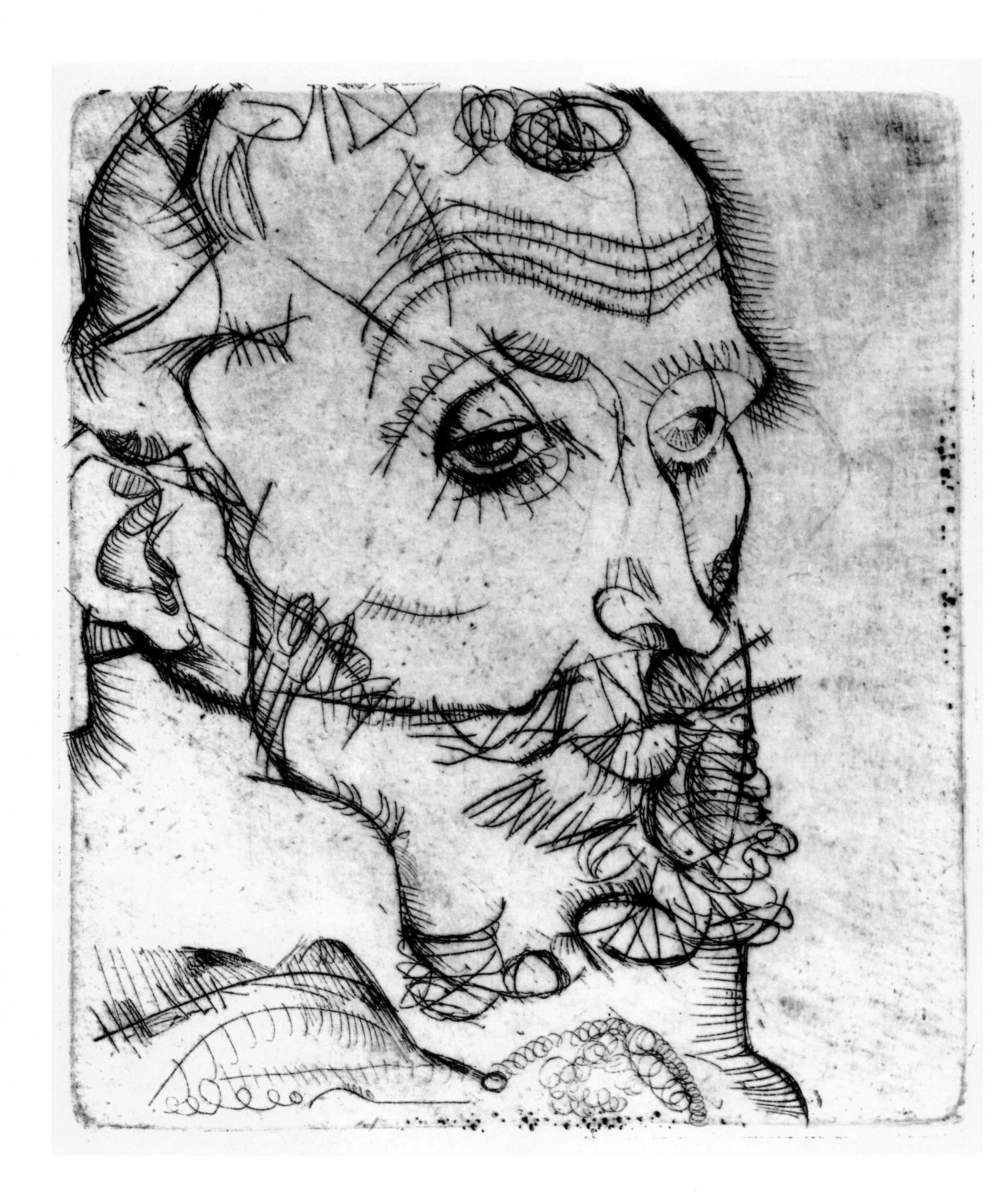

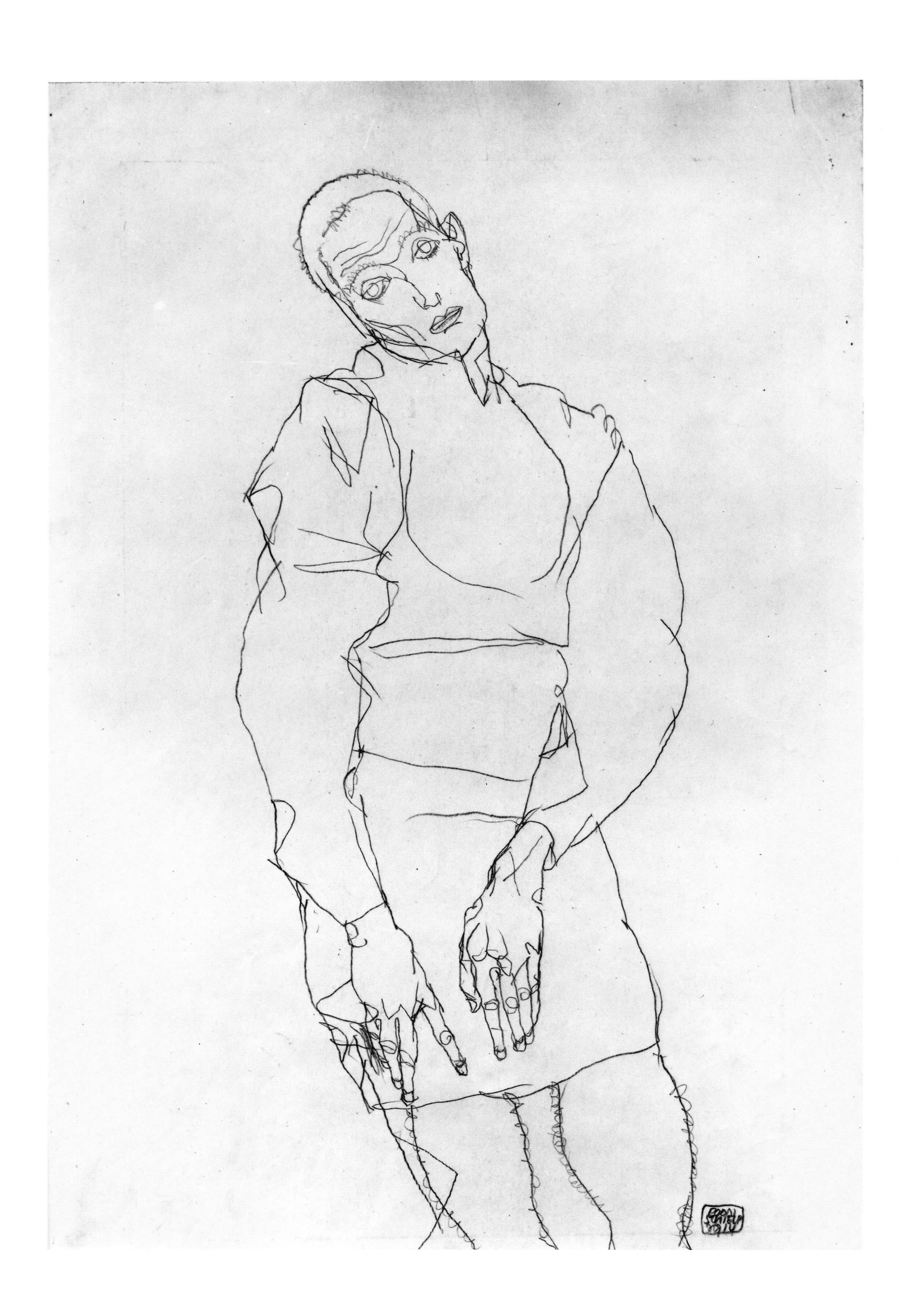

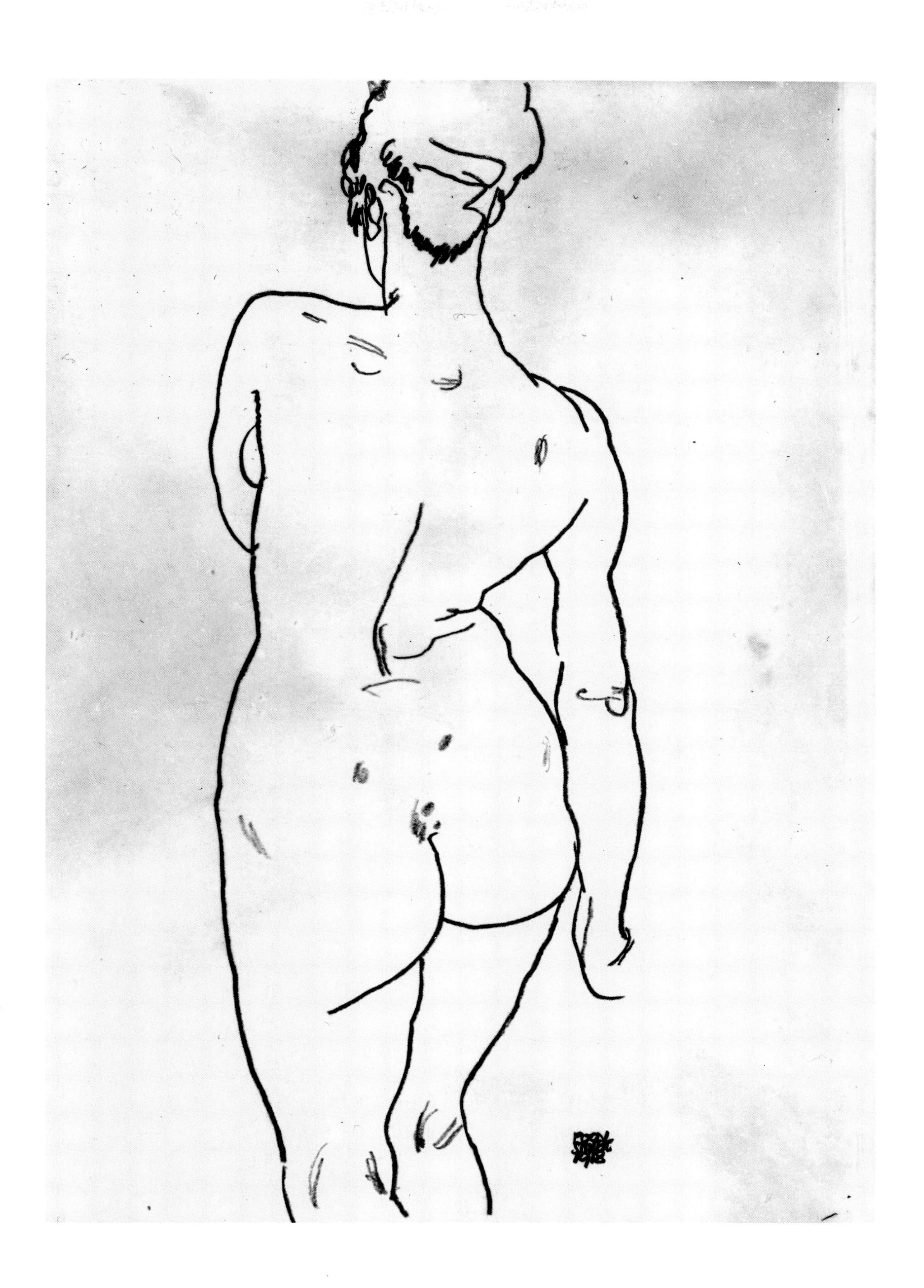

Self-Portrait with Red Shirt. 1914

Pencil and opaque colours on paper, 48 x 32 cm
Sammlung Hans Dichand, Vienna

Edith Schiele, Standing. 1915
Oil on canvas, 180 x 110.5 cm
Haags Gemeentemuseum, The Hague

1915

Death and Girl (Self-Portrait with Walli). 1915
Oil on canvas, 150 x 180 cm
Österreichische Galerie, Vienna

The Mill. 1916

Oil on canvas, 109 x 140 cm

Niederösterreichisches Landesmuseum, Vienna

Krumau Landscape. 1916

Oil on canvas, 110 x 140.5 cm

Neue Galerie der Stadt Linz, Wolfgang-Gurlitt-Museum

EGON
SCHIELE
1916

Sunflowers. 1917

Coloured drawing, 46 x 29.8 cm
Graphische Sammlung Albertina, Vienna

Four Trees. 1917

Oil on canvas, 110.5 x 141 cm

Österreichische Galerie, Vienna

The Artist's Wife. 1917

Pencil and opaque colours, 46 x 29.7 cm
Graphische Sammlung Albertina, Vienna

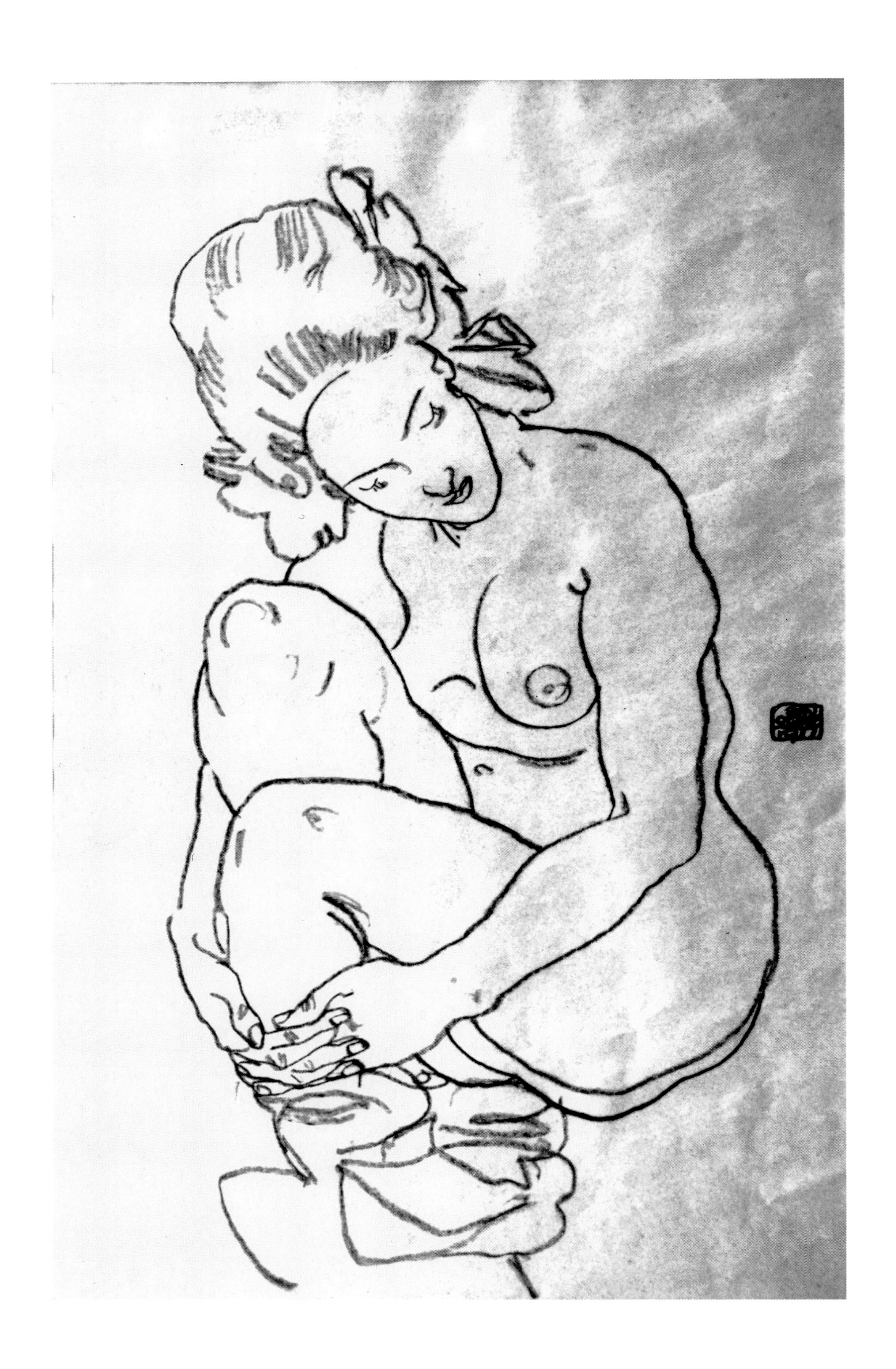

PARIS GÜTERSLOH

Sitting Woman with Legs Drawn up. 1917
Black crayon and opaque colours, 46 x 30 cm
National Gallery, Prague

Mother with Two Children. 1917

Oil on canvas, 150 x 158.7 cm
Österreichische Galerie, Vienna

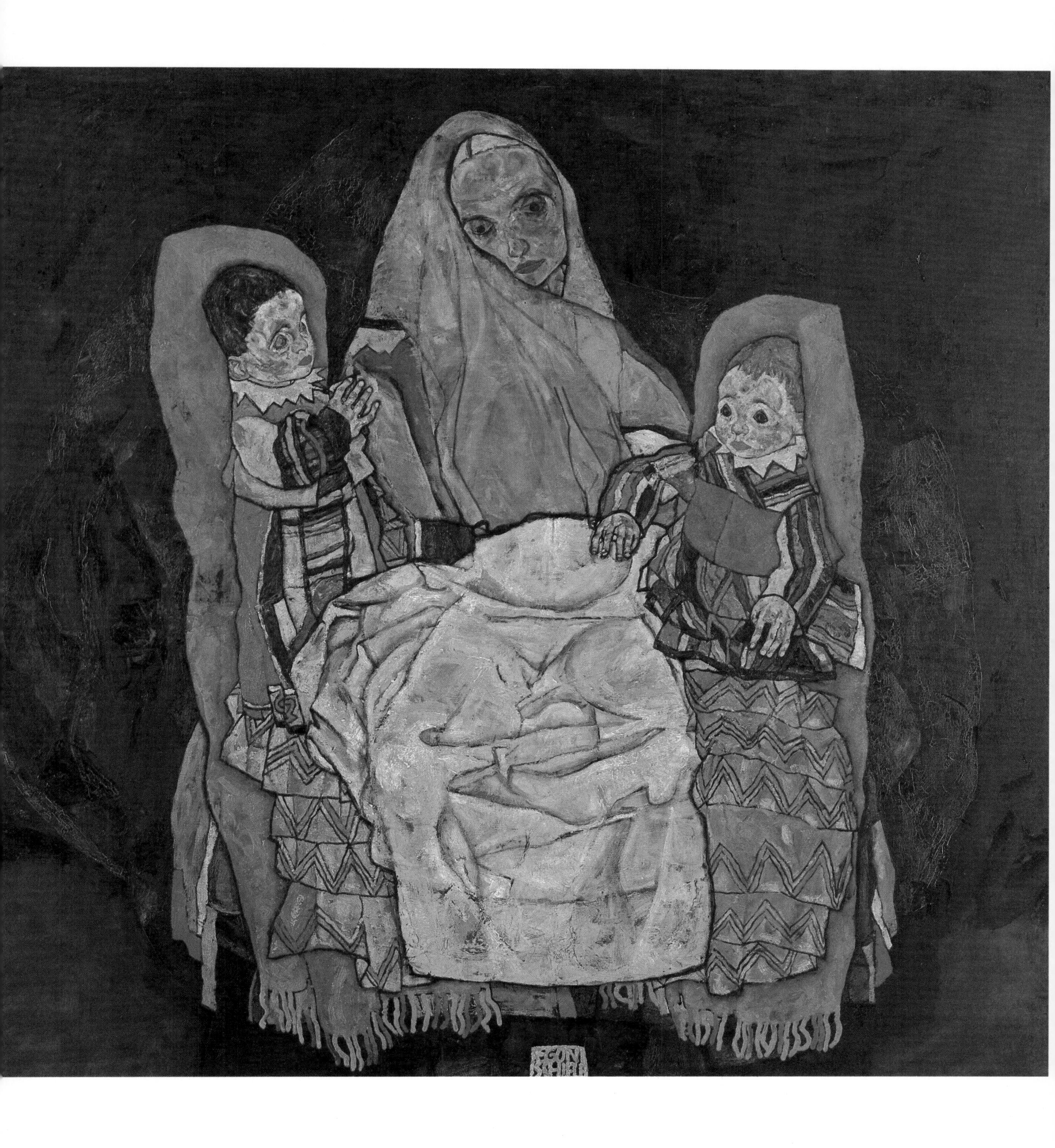

Portrait of Edith Schiele, Sitting. 1917/18
Oil on canvas, 140 x 110.5 cm
Österreichische Galerie, Vienna

The Family. 1918
Oil on canvas, 149.7 x 160 cm
Österreichische Galerie, Vienna

TABLE OF ILLUSTRATIONS

Photographic Acknowledgements:
Residenz Vlg., Salzburg: 31
Hessisches Landesmuseum, Darmstadt: 33
Foto Fürböck, Graz: 49
Artothek J. Hinrichs, Planeg: 55, 69, 95, 99
Hans Dichand, Wien: 57, 71, 77, 83, 93
Kunsthaus Zürich: 59
Staatsgalerie, Stuttgart: 81
Österreichische Galerie, Wien: 97, 121
Staatliche Graphische Sammlung, München: 60, 108
Nationalmuseum Stockholm: 65, 86
Graphische Sammlung Albertina, Wien: 36, 38, 40, 42, 43, 64, 66, 67, 84, 85, 87, 88, 89, 109, 111, 113, 114, 115
Historisches Museum, Wien: 39, 41, 61, 62, 63, 90, 91, 110, 112
Archiv Berghaus Verlag